YOU CHOOSE
BOOKS
Historical Eras

P9-CAO-579

ANCIENT EGYPT

An Interactive History Adventure

by Heather Adamson

Consultant:
Leo Depuydt
Professor, Department of Egyptology
and Ancient Western Asian Studies
Brown University
Providence, Rhode Island

Capstone
press®

Mankato, Minnesota

You Choose Books are published by Capstone Press,
151 Good Counsel Drive, P.O. Box 669, Mankato, Minnesota 56002.
www.capstonepub.com

Library of Congress Cataloging-in-Publication Data
Adamson, Heather, 1974–

Ancient Egypt : an interactive history adventure / by Heather Adamson.
p. cm. — (You choose books)
Summary: "Describes the life and times of the era known as ancient Egypt. The readers'
choices reveal the historical details of life as a pyramid builder in the Old Kingdom, life as an artist
in the New Kingdom, and life as a soldier or royal servant in the Ptolemaic Period" — Provided
by publisher.
Includes bibliographical references and index.
ISBN 978-1-4296-3415-1 (library binding)
ISBN 978-1-4296-3906-4 (pbk.)
1. Egypt — Civilization — To 332 B.C. — Juvenile literature. 2. Egypt — Social life and
customs — To 332 B.C. — Juvenile literature. I. Title. II. Series.
DT61.A35 2010
932 — dc22
2009002759

Editorial Credits
Megan Peterson, editor; Juliette Peters, set designer; Veronica Bianchini, book designer;
Kim Brown, illustrator; Wanda Winch, media researcher

Photo Credits
Alamy/Trip, 46; Art Life Images/J.D. Dallet, 6; Art Resource, N.Y./©British Museum, 54, 60; The
Bridgeman Art Library/Ancient Art and Architecture Collection Ltd./Private Collection/Building the
Pyramids, English School, 19; The Bridgeman Art Library/Giraudon/Bust of Agrippa, Louvre, Paris,
France, 77; The Bridgeman Art Library/©Look and Learn/Private Collection/Construction in Egypt,
English School, 17; The Bridgeman Art Library/©National Gallery of Scotland, Edinburgh, Scotland,
Cleopatra and Octavian, Gauffier, Louis, 96; The Bridgeman Art Library/The Stapleton Collection/
Private Collection/Stonemasons at Work, from a rare Record of Frescoes from Thebes, recorded
1819-1822 by Cailliaud, Frederick, 31; Compass Point Books/Peter Wilks, 45, 56, 59; Corbis/Gianni
Dagli Orti, 26; Getty Images Inc./The Bridgeman Art Library, 25, 40, 67; Getty Images Inc./The
Bridgeman Art Library/Frederick Arthur Bridgman, 89; Getty Images Inc./Hulton Archive, 81; Getty
Images Inc./Time Life Pictures/Mansell, 102; Jupiterimages Corporation, 100; North Wind Picture
Archives, 12, 75, 83; ©Petrie Museum of Egyptian Archaeology, University College London, UC63041,
33; Shutterstock/Connors Bros., 105; SuperStock, Inc./Christie's Images, 68; SuperStock, Inc./Corbis
Royalty-Free, cover; SuperStock, Inc./Superstock, 93; Wikipedia, public-domain image, 38

TABLE OF CONTENTS

About Your Adventure

YOU live in a time of breathtaking wealth and backbreaking labor. Will you experience ancient Egypt during the age of the pyramid builders, the mummy makers, or Queen Cleopatra?

In this book, you'll explore how the choices people made meant the difference between life and death. The events you'll experience happened to real people.

Chapter One sets the scene. Then you choose which path to read. Follow the directions at the bottom of each page. The choices you make will change your outcome. After you finish one path, go back and read the others for new perspectives and more adventures.

YOU CHOOSE the path
you take through history.

Ancient Egyptians built temples to worship their kings and the gods. Some temples still stand today.

THE GIFT OF THE NILE

Ancient Egypt was an era ahead of its time. Artists built magnificent buildings to honor the pharaohs and gods. An organized system of canals used water from the Nile River to grow enough crops for the country. A written language, called hieroglyphics, was widely used. A strong army protected ancient Egypt's massive wealth.

The Nile River was the lifeblood of ancient Egypt. Most ancient Egyptians were farmers. They depended on the annual Nile flood to grow crops such as wheat and barley. When the Nile flooded, harvests were plentiful. When the Nile didn't flood, the people of Egypt starved.

Turn the page.

Neighboring kingdoms wanted the Nile's power for themselves. Over the years, foreign rulers from Nubia, Syria, Persia, Greece, and Rome each had a turn controlling Egypt.

Just as the ancient Egyptians needed the Nile for physical survival, they needed the gods for spiritual survival. They believed in life after death. A proper burial was just as important as a good life. People worshipped the gods at home and in temples. The pharaoh was considered a living god. The pharaoh owned Egypt, including the land, its people, and all their possessions. Some pharaohs built large tombs called pyramids.

Life in ancient Egypt was hard. Many people died from accidents or disease. Soldiers fought and died protecting Egypt's borders. Workers toiled in the hot desert sun building monuments and tombs for royalty. Women often died during childbirth. People who lived past age 35 were considered old.

But the ancient Egyptians also enjoyed life. People attended parties and celebrations honoring the gods. They enjoyed music and dancing. Wealthy children attended school. Children and adults played games and spent time together.

Turn the page.

Appearance was very important to the ancient Egyptians. Men and women often shaved their heads to stay clean. Wealthier men and women wore wigs made of vegetable fibers or human hair. Both men and women wore eye paint. Most clothes were made of linen. Linen was lightweight and comfortable in the hot climate. Children often wore no clothes at all.

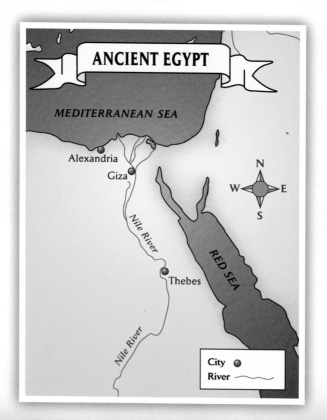

The historical era known as ancient Egypt began around 3100 BC. It ended in 30 BC, when Rome took over Egypt. Ancient Egypt was a time filled with adventure and mystery. The desert sands both preserve and hide secrets of the past. What will your journey to ancient Egypt reveal?

✦ To explore life during the pyramid-building age, turn to page **13**.

✦ To see what life was like during the tomb-building and mummy-making age, turn to page **41**.

✦ To experience life during the time of Cleopatra, turn to page **69**.

King Khufu often inspected the construction of his pyramid.

CHAPTER 2

THE PYRAMID BUILDERS

It's 2550 BC. King Khufu has ordered the construction of his pyramid tomb at a town called Giza. Khufu wants his pyramid to outshine all earlier pyramids. Khufu's father, King Snefru, built three pyramids. But one of them is sinking into the desert sands. Khufu's builders must avoid repeating past mistakes in order to honor Khufu and secure his place in the afterlife. It would be amazing to be associated with Khufu's pyramid in any way.

It's the season of *akhet*, when the Nile floods its banks. It will be months before it is *peret*, planting season. And it will be even longer until *shemu*, harvest season.

Turn the page.

Akhet is the perfect time to bring in supplies and temporary workers for Khufu's pyramid. A group of skilled workers already lives in Giza. With the river flooded, a harbor now lies just outside of Giza. Boatloads of cedar logs and copper tools are sailing in from Lebanon, Syria, and the Sinai Desert. Khufu's nephew Hemiunu is in charge of the construction. He will keep the work moving.

➤ To be a temporary worker at Giza, go to page 1!

➤ To be a skilled stonecutter at Giza, turn to page 2!

You live on a small family farm on the edge of the fertile land near the Nile River. It's the season of *akhet*. Canals hold back the water. When the river crests, the water flows down the canals to all the fields. The fields sit underwater for a season. Then the water recedes and leaves perfect soil for growing crops. Just inches beyond the green land, the desert sand piles up.

Your father speaks to you one morning after breakfast. "Our family has not contributed any laborers to Khufu's pyramid. I want you to go there and honor our family."

You have never been out of your village, but you are glad to go. Pyramid workers are greatly respected. You board a boat and travel to Giza.

Turn the page.

When you arrive at the Giza harbor, it is a sight beyond belief. Thousands of people are working on this enormous building project. The rapping of chisels on stone and workers shouting is an odd musical sound. You stare in awe at the pyramid. The lower part is already complete. Each side is 756 feet long.

You climb onto the dock and find the workers unloading the ship. "Where do I go to sign up for work?" you ask.

"Go into the workers' city," one of the men tells you. "Someone there will get you started." You thank him and walk to the workers' city. There are many tiny mud-brick homes and shops. Thick smoke billows from several bakeries and pottery shops. There is also a large bunker where temporary workers can sleep. You find the royal administration building and sign up for work.

The ancient Egyptians were skilled shipbuilders. They used the Nile River to travel.

You are excited when you learn about the rations. You will earn bread and beer each day. You can trade your extra rations for items in the city. Since you have no stonecutting skills, you are assigned to move the large blocks.

The limestone quarry is just south of the pyramid. You get up early each morning and walk to the quarry. You usually walk with Amosis. He also came from a farm. He reminds you of your brothers.

Turn the page.

At the limestone quarry, stonecutters use copper chisels and wooden wedges to cut out huge blocks of stone from the earth. Most blocks weigh 2.5 tons. A long, straight ramp rests against one side of the pyramid. To build the ramp, workers make two mud-brick walls. Then they fill the space between the walls with limestone chips and hard-packed earth. Your division of workers must move the blocks from the quarry and up the ramp to the pyramid.

"Hemiunu wants 300 blocks hauled to the pyramid each day," your boss orders when you arrive at work one morning. "We must move quickly."

Moving the blocks is hard work. Workers hoist each block onto a sled. Then a few other workers pull the sled. Once the sled gets going, it moves quickly. Sometimes the workers wrap ropes made of papyrus twine around the block. Then the workers pull it onto a short path of cedar logs. As the block is pulled, the logs roll forward. The blocks move fairly easily over the logs. Some workers must carry the logs from the back to the front of the rolling path.

Some historians believe workers used sleds to move the heavy blocks. Others think logs were used.

Turn the page.

"You are strong," Amosis says one day as you carry an empty sled back to the quarry. "I like to move blocks with you. I don't have to work so hard."

Division members work nine days in a row. They take turns having the 10th day off. You usually take your day off with Amosis. He hasn't been working here long either, but he knows how to get along in the city. After a few weeks, you and Amosis decide to trade your extra rations in the marketplace. Should you trade them for things your family needs, like tools for the farm? Or should you trade them for something you want, like a sleeping mat?

➤ To trade for items your family needs, go to page 2

➤ To trade for items you want, turn to page 2

You trade your rations for some new tools for the farm. Even though you are sore and covered in sand each night, you are glad to help your family. You hope the gods and the king will reward you and your family for your hard work.

You continue to work at the pyramid for a few months. It is almost harvest time. You know you should help your family with the harvest. But you like your life in Giza.

➤ *To keep working at the pyramid, turn to page 22.*

➤ *To return to the farm, turn to page 24.*

The harvest is small this year. You decide to stay at the pyramid. Besides, you are making friends and enjoying city life.

One day as your division lifts a block from the rolling log path to the pyramid ramp, a rope breaks. "Watch out!" Amosis yells. The block slides down the ramp. It knocks you down and lands on your right leg. You are dizzy.

"Quick! Move the stone," your boss says. "One, two, three. Lift!" The workers quickly heave the block from your leg. They put you on a wooden sled and take you to a doctor. You moan in pain as the doctor runs his hand along your leg.

"The bone is broken," he tells you. "I will set it back in place." First he makes a paste of spices and herbs. Then he spreads the paste on your leg. The smell is pleasant. It reminds you of your family's farm.

"Ahh!" you scream as the doctor pushes and pulls your bones back into place. Then he ties two boards around your leg and wraps it tightly with linen cloth.

After a few days of rest, you decide to go home. Your leg will take many weeks to heal. You will miss Amosis, but you are excited to see your family. They will be proud of your noble work.

THE END

To follow another path, turn to page 11.
To read the conclusion, turn to page 101.

"Welcome home," your father says when you return to the farm. It is good to see your family again. You have brought gifts of eye paint and spices for your family. These items are hard to find in the markets of your village.

Now is the season of *shemu*, or harvest. The men knock down the stalks with a tool called a sickle. Everyone, even the children, walks through the fields and gathers the stalks. Then animals walk over the stalks to separate the grain from the husks. A scribe writes down how much grain is harvested. He tells you what your family owes in taxes. It looks as though you will have enough to pay your taxes.

Scribes were among the few people in ancient Egypt who knew how to read and write.

When the harvest is over, you celebrate and tell stories. "Khufu's pyramid seemed to touch the heavens," you tell your family. Perhaps you will return to work on the pyramid again next year.

THE END

To follow another path, turn to page 11.
To read the conclusion, turn to page 101.

You trade some of your rations for a sleeping mat and a new linen kilt. You also trade for some black eye paint. Perhaps you will find some parties in the city to attend.

Your body aches at the end of each shift. But you like meeting people from all over Egypt. Soon, you spend all of your free time in the workers' city. You love to walk to the richer side of town. There you attend fancy parties and watch the hired singers and dancers. You keep most of your rations for yourself.

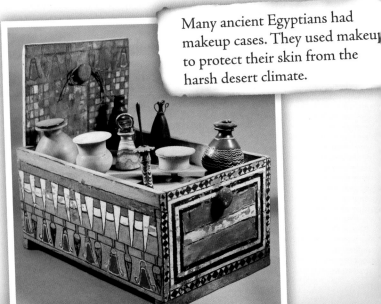

Many ancient Egyptians had makeup cases. They used makeup to protect their skin from the harsh desert climate.

After a few months at the pyramid, you arrive home to help with the harvest. But you did not know that a plague has hit this region. Your family didn't have enough goods to trade for vegetables, meat, or medicine. Many of them were weak. They died from the plague. You wonder if you could have saved your family by sending home goods or food. Your selfish actions haunt you for the rest of your life.

THE END

To follow another path, turn to page 11.
To read the conclusion, turn to page 101.

You have lived in Giza for most of your life. Your father was one of the first stonecutters at Khufu's pyramid. He taught you how to use the wedge and chisel.

"I can't believe you are ready to start work on Khufu's monument," your mother says the day you are to sign up for work. You are excited to earn your own rations of bread and beer each day.

You must decide if you will cut stone in the quarry or at the pyramid. In the quarry, stonecutters chisel out the large blocks from the sandy ledges. At the pyramid, workers smooth the blocks and level the surfaces. Each block must fit together perfectly.

→ *To cut stone in the quarry, go to page 2*

→ *To finish the stones at the pyramid, turn to page 3*

Most of the stone for Khufu's pyramid comes from a quarry right in Giza. A few choice stones of granite and white limestone come from Aswan and Tura. They are shipped on the Nile River to Giza.

Your job is to help cut the large blocks from the local quarry. When you get to the quarry, your boss hands you a hammer, wedge, and copper chisel. "Use the chisel to make holes along the edge of the block," he explains to you. "Then hammer the wooden wedges into the holes to get a clean break between the holes."

Turn the page.

The large pieces of rock must be cut to size and squared before being hauled to the pyramid site. It takes a lot of work with a hammer and chisel. Several people work together to smooth each block. You cut small pieces off until it is square. Clink. Clink. Clink. The sound rings in your brain. You must keep the blocks in order so they fit together at the pyramid.

Your division has about a dozen workers in it. Your division is part of a crew of 2,000 workers. There are two main crews working on the pyramid. The two crews are competing to see who will get their part of the pyramid put together better and faster. You like the other men in your division. You look out for one another. Thousands of other workers help make tools, build ramps, and prepare food.

Turn to page

Workers used hammers and copper chisels to smooth the rough pyramid blocks.

You get a job working on the pyramid. The blocks come from the quarry ready to fit together. You fit the blocks into place and make sure the top is perfectly level. To level each block, you stretch a string over the block's surface. Then you slide a stick under the string. The distance between the string and the block must be the same from one end of the string to the other. You use your hammer and chisel to smooth out any high spots.

Turn the page.

Your boss is impressed by how quickly you level each block. "How would you like a position with more responsibility?" he asks. He puts you to work on the angled blocks that form the pyramid's outer corner.

This work has a few more challenges. First you level the blocks. Then you use a wooden guide to angle the corners. The edges must be smooth. If all the blocks are not cut at the exact same angle, the pyramid's corner will look jagged. Your boss sees your hard work. When he hands out the day's rations, he surprises you with an offer.

"I have a daughter who is ready to marry," he tells you. "You can take her into your household. Then I will give you a promotion."

Archaeologists have found copper chisels used by the pyramid workers.

Your boss' daughter is of a higher class. If you marry her, you can become a division leader. You will receive more rations and be in charge of other workers. You may even earn a grave site right near the great pyramid of Khufu. But your family has had another girl in mind for you for a few years. She is pretty, and her family owns many cattle.

→ To refuse to marry, turn to page **34**.

→ To marry your boss' daughter, turn to page **36**.

You anger your boss by refusing his offer. He gives you fewer rations each day. You have enough to eat but not enough to trade for things like eye paint and furniture.

One day a worker has trouble getting two blocks to fit together. A tiny crack of light shines between them at one of the corners. "What kind of work is this?" your boss asks. "This is not fit for the gods."

"It must have been cut incorrectly at the quarry," you say. "I will fix it." You grab your hammer and chisel and scramble to the block.

"If you can cut stone so much better than the quarry workers, I will send you there to work," your boss says. You know he is taking this chance to get rid of you. You head off to the quarry to start work cutting blocks.

Today your division is cutting a stone block high up on a rock face. You are standing on a small rocky ledge as you work. Crack!

"Look out!" a worker yells. It is too late. The ledge breaks away. You fall down into the quarry pit below. The last thing you see is a large pile of stones falling on top of you. You are crushed to death.

Your division carries your body back to the workers' city. You are not buried in the cemetery for temporary workers. Instead, you are buried in a small mastaba. Scrap pieces of beautiful stone cover your tomb. The gods are sure to notice your grave. Your spirit will find you quickly, and you will celebrate in the afterlife.

THE END

To follow another path, turn to page 11.
To read the conclusion, turn to page 101.

You meet your boss' daughter, Nebet. She is pretty and kind. You decide to marry her. She moves into your family's house. You must provide her with food and clothing. She likes fancy wigs and perfumes. She also enjoys city life.

At work, you now supervise a few divisions of workers. "The workers must set a stone in place every two minutes," your boss explains. As the supervisor, you examine your divisions' work and give the workers their rations. Supervisors receive more rations.

You must decide what to do with your increased rations. You could get new wigs or throw a nice celebration. Or you can use the rations to reward your workers.

→ To keep your rations, go to page 3

→ To reward your workers, turn to page 3

"The workers get plenty of rations," you explain to Nebet one night at supper. "Why should I give them mine as well?"

You use your increased rations to throw large parties. But your workers are getting angry. They notice your new eye paint, expensive wigs, and gold amulets. Fed up with your selfishness, they begin doing poor work.

Your boss blames you for your workers' actions. He fires you and throws you out of Giza. Nebet divorces you. She marries your brother, who takes over your job. He doesn't make the same mistakes. His workers are happy, and he becomes rich. You spend the rest of your days wandering from village to village, taking odd jobs. It is a lonely life.

THE END

To follow another path, turn to page 11.
To read the conclusion, turn to page 101.

"You honor Khufu and the gods with your hard work," you tell your divisions at the end of a long, hot day. You reward them with extra bread and beer. In return, your divisions work harder and faster.

Hemiunu notices your hard work. "You are a skilled supervisor. Would you help build Khufu's burial chamber?"

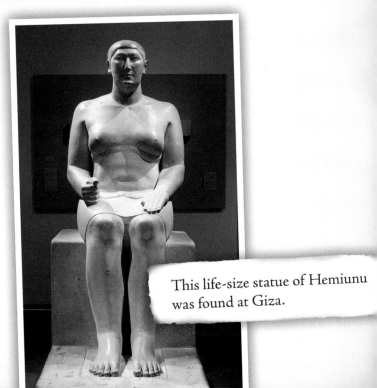

This life-size statue of Hemiunu was found at Giza.

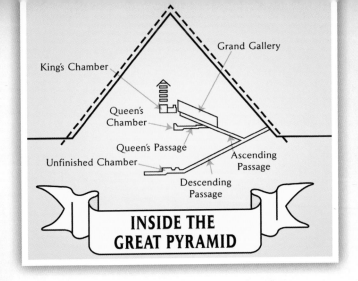

INSIDE THE GREAT PYRAMID

"It will be an honor," you reply. Only the best pyramid workers are chosen to help build the king's chamber. This small room will one day hold the king's coffin. You supervise 200 men as they pull a huge granite block up the pyramid ramp. Then you make sure the stone is placed correctly on the pyramid. It is your proudest moment. You are certain to be rewarded in the afterlife.

THE END

To follow another path, turn to page 11.
To read the conclusion, turn to page 101.

King Akhenaten and
Queen Nefertiti built the
new royal city of Akhetaten.

CHAPTER 3

TOMBS AND MUMMIES

It's 1320 BC. You are an artist living in Thebes. Until a few years ago, you lived in the royal city of Akhetaten. King Akhenaten built the new city, abandoning the capital of Thebes. Instead of worshipping the traditional Egyptian gods, Akhenaten believed in only one god, the sun god Aten. Akhenaten forced his new religious beliefs on the people of Egypt.

In Akhetaten, you worked as an apprentice to an artist. He trained you to make artwork and statues of King Akhenaten and his wife, Queen Nefertiti. It was an amazing time to be an artist. You had freedom to create new things. Other pharaohs told artists when the royalty could be drawn and how the art should look.

Turn the page.

In Akhetaten, you observed the royal family as they worshipped, ate, and relaxed. You added backgrounds and nature to your pieces. The faces could even show expressions.

But in the years since King Akhenaten's death, you have lived through confusing times. No one knows what became of Queen Nefertiti. Control of Egypt has passed through many hands. Akhenaten's young son, Tutankhamen, is now the king of Egypt. His new government is erasing Akhenaten's ideas. The officials ordered the city of Akhetaten closed. They returned art and religion to the traditional ways.

You must now choose a different path for your life. The new rulers are beginning work on their burial chambers in the Valley of the Kings. They need tomb painters. You are skilled in this area. But you are not sure you can trust this new government. You could also take your skills to the marketplace. You could become wealthy by making idols, statues, and masks. People need these items for their own tombs.

➤ To work in the Valley of the Kings, turn to page **44**.

➤ To use your talents in the marketplace, turn to page **57**.

The Valley of the Kings is on the west bank of the Nile River near Thebes. For hundreds of years, Egyptian kings have chosen to be buried there. Tall cliffs and a narrow entryway make the valley difficult for tomb robbers to enter.

You arrive at the workers' village, which is southeast of the Valley of the Kings. A wall of mud bricks surrounds the small village of about 100 people. The men build and decorate the royal tombs in the valley. The women take care of the children, and some sell goods in the marketplace. Workers are paid in grain, fish, and vegetables.

Two foremen oversee the tomb-building projects. Each foreman is in charge of his own gang. Scribes take attendance and keep track of all materials used to build and furnish the tombs.

"You will paint a mural in a nobleman's burial chamber," your foreman tells you when you arrive at the valley.

Tomb artists used grids to make sure the artwork was accurate.

You enter the dark tomb carrying a lamp made of linen strips and animal fat. The plastered walls of the chamber are covered in red drawings. It is your job to add paint to the drawings.

You begin painting a mural of Osiris, the god of the underworld. He is shown as a human mummy with black skin. He wears a white crown with feathers and holds a curved stick.

A scribe named Khonsu also works in the burial chamber. He is carving an inscription above the entryway. "Do you want to come to a party at my uncle's house tonight?" he asks. "I hear the vizier might come."

Turn the page.

This tomb belonged to a worker in the Valley of the Kings. He shared his tomb with his wife, their children, and grandchildren.

"The vizier?" If the highest official in Egypt is coming, it must be an important party.

"Yes," Khonsu laughs. "If you piled up the *debens* of gold my uncle has spent for this celebration, it would probably fill this room."

You are excited about the invitation. You would need to leave work early to be ready for a party like that. But today is your first day at work. You want to impress your foreman.

⇒ To stay at work, go to page 4

⇒ To go to the party, turn to page 5

"I'm going to keep painting," you tell Khonsu. The burial chamber will require many hours to complete. You want to be certain the painting is finished before the nobleman dies. It will ensure him a safe journey to the next life. If you work hard enough, you might be promoted to paint King Tut's tomb.

"Suit yourself," Khonsu says. He leaves you alone in the chamber. As you are painting, you hear a loud snapping sound overhead. You look up as long cracks splinter the ceiling. If the ceiling falls, you could become trapped. But if you try to run, you might be crushed to death by the falling rocks.

→ To stay where you are, turn to page 48.

→ To run, turn to page 49.

Pieces of the ceiling crash to the floor. You duck, shielding your head with your arms. When the dust settles, you hold out your lamp with an unsteady hand. Several large, heavy stones block the chamber's door.

"Help!" you shout. "In here!" No one answers. You are trapped. The other workers will think the falling ceiling killed you. No one will come looking for you. You hope to have better luck in the next life.

THE END

To follow another path, turn to page 11.
To read the conclusion, turn to page 101.

You pick up your lamp and run out of the chamber. You look back just as pieces of the ceiling crash to the floor. Huge stones now block the chamber's door. As you catch your breath, someone grabs your shoulder. You turn around to face Khonsu.

"Are you all right?" he asks. "I was just outside the tomb when I heard a loud rumble."

"I'm fine," you tell him. You wipe the dust from your eyes. "The workers must have tunneled too close to an existing tomb. The ceiling had a weak spot."

Khonsu smiles. "Now you can come to my uncle's party tonight."

Turn the page.

An opportunity like this is too good to pass up. Who knows what you might see at such an important party? You head home and put on your finest white kilt and several amulets.

You walk through the village to the party. Khonsu's uncle lives in an elegant house. People stand on the flat rooftop, talking and laughing. Music swells from the courtyard. As you enter the gate, a servant gives you a scented wax cone for your head. Your body heat will melt the cone, releasing its perfume. You put it on your head and join the party.

The food is fantastic. There are roasted meats, fish, and plenty of watermelon, cucumbers, and bread. Your glass is filled with beer or wine as soon as it is empty. You sit with Khonsu in the moonlit courtyard. He talks of all the riches being placed in the tomb you are painting.

"The nobleman is not even dead yet, and already there are boxes filled with gold," Khonsu says.

"I saw a room with jugs of spices and granite sculptures of the gods," you add.

"The royal officials don't need all of that," Khonsu says. "They are wasteful and greedy. Look at what they did to the beautiful city of Akhetaten. I worked many months on a temple there. They have smashed most of it down."

"It does seem a shame," you agree as you sip your wine.

51

"I am going to take some of what I am still owed for my work. A few gold amulets will never be missed. Do you want to help me?" Khonsu asks.

➤ To do honest work, turn to page 52.

➤ To steal from the tomb, turn to page 53.

"I don't dare anger the gods," you tell Khonsu. You leave the party before he can argue.

You decide to work late the next night. You don't want anyone to think you are involved in any crimes. Khonsu has been fun to work with, but you decide to stay away from him for a while.

Your foreman soon notices your great work. He rewards you with extra grain. He gives you more projects in other chambers. After a few years of service, you are given your own small tomb for when you die. It is a high honor for you and your family.

THE END

To follow another path, turn to page 11.
To read the conclusion, turn to page 101.

The next day, Khonsu takes a few gold amulets and puts them in his palette with his tools on top. Scribes always carry their palettes with them. The palette holds their pens, ink, and carving tools. If anyone stops him, he will show them his tools.

You come up with a plan to steal some small statues. You paint a few statues and rub off the paint in places. Then you pack them in a small crate. You wait while Khonsu goes out ahead of you. Khonsu is not stopped. You leave the tomb a bit later. The guard stops you. "What are you doing with those?" he demands, pointing to the statues in your crate.

→ To fix the statues and put them back, turn to page **54**.

→ To try to keep the statues, turn to page **55**.

Some ancient Egyptians placed *shabti* figures in their tombs. They believed these figures would help them in the afterlife.

"These statues are damaged," you explain. "I need to repair them outside where they will dry quickly." The guard looks at the statues. Then he shows you a good place to work. The paint dries quickly. You put the statues back inside the tomb.

You decide to earn your riches by doing honest work. Khonsu raids a few more tombs and then leaves the village. You later hear that Khonsu was arrested near Giza. You are glad you escaped the same fate.

54

THE END

To follow another path, turn to page 11.
To read the conclusion, turn to page 101.

"I need to take these statues to my shop to repair them," you lie.

The guard waves over one of the scribes. Together they read the scribe's list of burial items. Then the scribe whispers something to the guard and walks away.

"The scribe says you added paint to these statues," the guard tells you. He arrests you. You are taken across the river into Thebes. A guard whips your arms and legs until you confess. Then you are brought back to the site of your crime. The vizier waits for you there. He listens to your story.

Turn the page.

Tomb robbing was common in ancient Egypt. Robbers often tunneled their way into the tomb

"Did you act alone?" the vizier asks.

"Yes," you reply. You don't want Khonsu to be punished. You are convicted of your crime. Guards drag you to the edge of town. A short stick stands in the ground with a sharpened end. The guards push you onto the stick. You are left to die. Your body will be a warning to all who think of raiding the riches of a royal tomb.

THE END

To follow another path, turn to page 11.
To read the conclusion, turn to page 101.

You decide to set up shop here in Thebes. You make statues and amulets of the gods and sell them in the marketplace. One day a man named Hay stops to look at your wares.

"These are magnificent," he says. "How would you like to work with me at my embalming shop? I could use someone to decorate the sarcophagi and make masks for my customers."

Egyptians embalm or preserve dead bodies by making them into mummies. They believe there is another world after death. But before a person can take part in the afterlife, the parts of the soul must find their way back to the body. Preserved bodies are easier for the gods and soul to recognize. But to make it even easier for the gods and soul, masks and artwork are placed on the body and in the tomb. Large chests called sarcophagi hold the mummified bodies.

Turn the page.

"An artist can have no nobler task," you tell Hay. You pack up your things and follow Hay to his shop.

Embalming is expensive. Hay does a lot of business. Most people have set aside much of their wealth for their death or the death of a family member. Many will have artwork or masks made long before they are dead.

No one wants their body to end up filled with oil and salt and buried in the sand. Hay's best customers are embalmed by priests. You watch as the priests embalm the body of a nobleman. First the priests make a small cut on the abdomen. They remove and embalm the organs. You carve and paint a special jar to hold each organ. The jars will be placed in the tomb with the mummy.

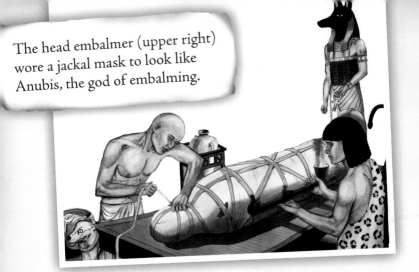

The head embalmer (upper right) wore a jackal mask to look like Anubis, the god of embalming.

"The brain is not an important organ," one of the priests explains. He slides a long hook up the nose. Then he pulls out the brain in bits. "The heart is the seat of wisdom," the priest continues. He leaves it in place. Then the priests fill the body with salt to dry it out. Finally, the priests fill the body with fine spices and wrap it in strips of linen. They even wrap the fingers and toes separately so the nails don't fall off. The mask is placed on the wrapped body. The finest masks are made of solid gold. The entire process takes 70 days.

Turn the page.

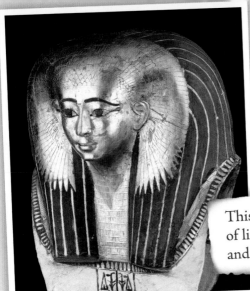

This death mask was made of linen stiffened with plaster and covered in gold.

One day as you are painting gold trim on a mask, Hay tells you, "That layer of gold looks nice. One would think the whole thing was solid gold."

Suddenly you have an idea. When Hay sells people the solid gold death masks, you could make them out of heavy plaster and use a thin layer of gold. You could keep the extra gold for yourself.

❧ To cheat Hay's customers, go to page 6

❧ To do honest work, turn to page 6

Not only are you able to gain a lot of money by only using a layer of gold, you also save time. You are able to take on more of Hay's projects.

You try to be careful with your new riches. You trade for a nice wig and kilt, but you are careful not to wear too much jewelry. You don't want people to suspect you are cheating them.

You are afraid that Hay knows what you are doing. Earlier, he stopped by the workshop. "You are doing some interesting work," he told you. "I would like to meet with you later to talk about it."

→ *To meet with Hay, turn to page 62.*

→ *To run away, turn to page 63.*

You decide to meet with Hay. He comes in holding one of your more recent masks. "I see you have been skimping on the gold," he says. He takes the mask and throws it on the ground. Smash! The heavy plaster you coated with gold breaks into pieces.

"Do you have any other ideas?" Hay asks. "I think we need to be partners in our schemes." Hay's not angry. He's impressed.

"I do have a few more ideas," you tell him. Together, you and Hay come up with many ideas to cheat people. Your favorite is selling embalmed gifts of food. But the food is really old wood wrapped in linen. You are never caught. You become rich enough to marry a beautiful girl. You live in a large house with your many children.

62

THE END

To follow another path, turn to page 11.
To read the conclusion, turn to page 101.

You gather your tools and a few granite statues and place them in a large crate. You try to decide where to go. Should you leave Egypt? Maybe you could travel down the Nile River and set up shop in a small farming town.

Smash! You turn and see that Hay has entered the shop. He shattered one of your masks on the ground. It is clearly not made of solid gold. "You swindler!" he cries. "You thief!"

Hay takes you to the judge. The judge finds you guilty of your crime. You are ordered to pay back all of the stolen gold plus heavy fines. To work off your debt, you are given to Hay and his family. You spend the rest of your life as a household servant.

THE END

To follow another path, turn to page 11.
To read the conclusion, turn to page 101.

You decide to do honest work. Those caught stealing must give back what they stole and pay heavy fines. Some are even tortured or killed.

Soon after, word spreads that King Tut has been injured. He isn't healing. He will die. Tut has been pharaoh since he was 9 years old. He is now 19. Everyone thought he would celebrate a Sed Festival. This celebration is held for those who rule for 30 years.

One day, you are decorating a sarcophagus when Hay brings you some happy news. "You are one of the artists chosen to make art for the king's tomb," he tells you. This is a great honor. You could carve a gold statue of one of the gods. But that could take weeks. You won't be able to serve many customers. You might lose business.

➤ To make a simple statue, go to page 65

➤ To make a gold statue, turn to page 66

Business is business. You decide to make a simple granite statue of Amun, the creator god. You spend a few days carving Amun's flat crown with two feathers on top. When it is finished, you are pleased with your work. You give the statue to Hay, who takes it to Tut's tomb.

Hay returns from the tomb a few days later. "They had many granite statues of Amun," he explains. "They didn't need any extras." Hay gives you back your statue. You wish you had taken the time to create something special for your king.

THE END

To follow another path, turn to page 11.
To read the conclusion, turn to page 101.

You decide to make a gold statue of Isis, a protector goddess. Isis is shown as a queen. On her head, Isis wears the sign for "throne." You spend several weeks carving the statue. You polish it to a shining brilliance. The work is so beautiful, you are asked to make King Tut's death mask.

This is a great honor. You use more than 20 pounds of solid gold to make the mask. You add colored glass and jewels. You represent the two kingdoms of Egypt with a falcon and a serpent. You trim the mask with black. On the back, you carve spells to help Tut in the underworld. You are proud of your work. The king will surely remember you in the next life.

THE END

To follow another path, turn to page 11.
To read the conclusion, turn to page 101.

King Tut's death mask is the most recognized artifact from ancient Egypt.

Queen Cleopatra was the first Ptolemaic ruler to learn the Egyptian language.

CHAPTER 4

THE END OF THE PHARAOHS

You live in Egypt in 31 BC. Things haven't been all that great since Greek leader Alexander the Great conquered Egypt in 332 BC. General Ptolemy took over after Alexander died. For the last 300 years, Ptolemy's family line has ruled Egypt. Cleopatra VII, the daughter of Ptolemy XII, took the throne in 51 BC. She was just 18 years old. She lives in Alexandria, a beautiful port city on the Mediterranean Sea.

You are worried about Egypt. Cleopatra spent a few years living in Rome with Roman dictator Julius Caesar. She even had a son with him, named Caesarion. While Cleopatra was gone, she didn't see the effects of a few years of bad harvests or a weak army.

Turn the page.

In 44 BC, Caesar was assassinated by a group of Roman senators. A civil war broke out in Rome. Cleopatra had to flee back to Alexandria.

In his will, Caesar did not leave his wealth or ruling name to Caesarion. He left nothing to his faithful second-in-command, Mark Antony. Instead, he left everything to a distant relative, Octavian. Together, Antony and Octavian defeated Caesar's murderers. Then Octavian made an agreement with Antony. The agreement gave Antony control of the eastern part of the Roman Empire.

Antony invited Cleopatra to meet with him. He wanted Egypt's loyalty. Cleopatra arrived at their meeting in her royal boat.

Dressed like a goddess and perched under a canopy of gold tissue, Cleopatra impressed Antony. He fell in love with her. Over the next few years, Cleopatra and Antony had three children together.

Octavian warned Rome that Cleopatra and Antony planned to take sole control of the Roman Empire. In 32 BC, the Roman Senate declared war against Cleopatra.

Cleopatra is determined to make Egypt great again. She is building new temples and fixing the canals. She even lowered farm taxes to increase grain production. With Cleopatra's wealth, Egypt's shipbuilding skill, and Antony's military leadership, you hope Cleopatra will be able to defeat Octavian.

→ To join the Egyptian military, turn to page 72.

→ To serve Cleopatra as one of her servants, turn to page 88.

It is September of 31 BC. Mark Antony, Queen Cleopatra, and their fleet of 300 ships have been stationed along the Ionian Sea at Actium since winter. Actium is a small town on the coast of western Greece. It sits on the south side of the entrance to the Ambracian Gulf. The gulf's entrance is less than half a mile wide. Antony's men built huge towers on either side of the gulf. From the towers, they can launch rocks and fireballs at enemy ships that try to enter the gulf.

Octavian's men are camped 5 miles north of the gulf's entrance. More than 400 Roman ships have trapped Antony's ships at Actium. Antony's fleet cannot leave without battling Octavian's men. And Antony has a shortage of rowers for his ships. He could abandon his fleet and lead the army into eastern Greece. He could also fight a sea battle. Either choice will be dangerous. Antony needs brave fighters.

→ *To become an army soldier, turn to page* **74**.

→ *To become a naval archer, turn to page* **82**.

You are a soldier under the command of Canidius Crassus. Actium is a dreary place. The poor soil won't grow crops. There is no fresh water. Many soldiers become sick with fever, vomiting, and diarrhea. The disease spreads from soldier to soldier, killing many.

You join a group of men who are gathered around Crassus. "Antony is not a naval man," Crassus says. "He should have listened to me and fought the battle on land."

"Look!" a soldier yells, pointing to the sea. "Antony has set some of our ships on fire!"

It is a sickening sight. Many perfectly good ships light up the sea like candles. "Why is Antony burning our ships?" you ask.

"Too many rowers have died or deserted the navy," Crassus explains. "There aren't enough men to row all the ships. Now Octavian won't be able to use our empty ships against us."

The remaining ships, led by Antony and Cleopatra, will row out to sea the next day. They will battle with Octavian's fleet. But you are too hungry to care. Octavian cut off the supply of grain from Egypt. You haven't eaten for days. Many soldiers have starved to death.

Mark Antony (pictured) was a cavalry officer under Julius Caesar.

Turn the page.

You wander off in search of food or water. You stumble upon a group of soldiers. They are huddled together and whispering.

"What's going on?" you ask one of the soldiers.

"Antony and Cleopatra are greatly outnumbered," he tells you. "Octavian will win the battle. We have decided to defect to the Romans. Will you join us?"

➝ To desert Antony and join the Roman, go to page 7

➝ To stay with Antony's army, turn to page 8

General Agrippa (pictured) was Octavian's naval advisor and lifelong friend.

You recognize a losing battle when you see one. You and the other soldiers sneak out of camp in the middle of the night. You travel to Octavian's camp and surrender.

"Come with me," a Roman soldier says. He leads you and the other soldiers to General Agrippa's tent. Agrippa is the leader of the Roman Navy.

Turn the page.

"What can you tell me about Antony's plans?" he asks.

"The soldiers are sick and starving. And Antony has a shortage of rowers," you explain. "He burned his extra ships to keep them out of Octavian's hands."

Agrippa uses your information to form a new attack plan. Tomorrow, the Romans will tire out Antony's rowers and attack his ships with flaming arrows.

The next day, a Roman soldier asks you to help row one of Octavian's ships. You climb aboard and join the other oarsmen. On Agrippa's command, you and the entire Roman fleet row out into open water. You look back at the shore. Antony's fleet looks small.

You learn that Agrippa is a talented general. When Antony's tired rowers reach open water, Agrippa orders the Roman boats to lurch forward. Two or three Roman boats attack each of Antony's ships.

In the middle of the battle, Cleopatra's squadron of 60 ships flees. Antony abandons his fleet and follows her. It is a good thing you defected to the Romans. They easily defeat Antony's remaining ships. Within one week, all of Antony's men have surrendered or been killed. You are grateful to be alive.

Egypt becomes part of the Roman Empire, which stretches over most of the known world. Octavian becomes Emperor Caesar Augustus. You serve him the rest of your days.

THE END

To follow another path, turn to page 11.
To read the conclusion, turn to page 101.

"I cannot abandon Antony," you tell the soldiers. You stay with the Egyptian Army. There is still a chance Antony and Cleopatra will defeat Octavian's fleet. Then the army can safely sail to Rome and crush Octavian's land forces.

The next day, Antony and Cleopatra lead their ships into open water. You watch as Octavian's smaller and faster ships surround Antony's bigger ships. Roman sailors pour onto the decks of Antony's ships. They kill many of Antony's men with spears.

Suddenly, Cleopatra's squadron of 60 ships flees from battle. Then Antony abandons his men and sails away to join her. By nightfall, all of Antony's ships have been overtaken or surrendered.

Octavian became the first emperor of Rome in 27 BC.

"We will march into eastern Greece and wait for Antony," Crassus tells you and the other soldiers. But Crassus flees in the night. You and the other soldiers decide to join Octavian's forces. You serve in the Roman Army the rest of your days.

THE END

To follow another path, turn to page 11.
To read the conclusion, turn to page 101.

You are an archer in the navy commanded by Mark Antony. You have been hiding out along the Ionian Sea since winter. Many men are sick with fever, vomiting, and diarrhea. Octavian's forces have cut off most of your grain supply. There is not enough food or fresh water for all the men camped in this small, swampy bay.

You serve on one of Antony's large ships, called a quinquereme. This type of ship is big and heavy. The ship's hull is made of large pieces of wood bolted together with iron. On the prow, or front of the boat, is a large bronze battering ram. It is used to slam into and destroy enemy ships.

One night as you walk on the deck of your ship, you spot flames on one of Antony's ships. Soon you realize that several ships are burning.

Once the opposing fleets came together, sailors set enemy ships on fire.

You find another sailor and drag him up onto the deck. "Look! We must do something to save our fleet!" you yell.

"Antony has decided to fight a sea battle. And there is a shortage of rowers," the sailor explains. "He ordered the ships to be burned. He doesn't want Octavian to take our empty ships."

Many men have deserted the army and navy. Others have died. Some have even joined the Romans. But you are loyal to Egypt and Cleopatra.

Turn the page.

The next day, Antony's fleet moves out in two lines. Cleopatra's squadron of 60 ships follows behind them. The oarsmen on your ship row out to sea where Octavian's fleet of lighter and faster ships awaits. You climb onto your ship's tower. Your ship slices through the water as the rowers pick up speed. As soon as you are close enough, you will shoot arrows at the enemy boats. Other sailors will launch stones with catapults and slingshots.

The ship ahead of you rams a Roman boat with a thud instead of a crack. It is unable to damage the Roman boat. Two more Roman ships swarm the boat. Roman sailors use grappling hooks to pull the boat close. Then they climb onto the ship's deck, armed with spears and torches. They kill most of the men on board and start the ship on fire.

Your rowers are weak and tired. And your boat is losing speed. Will your ship be overtaken?

"Cleopatra's ships are leaving the battle!" a sailor yells. You watch helplessly as Cleopatra's ships escape through the center of the battle. Your section of ships is packed tightly together. Antony's ship is engaged in battle. You hear him shout that he needs a boat to take him out after Cleopatra. Does Antony plan to flee the battle? Or does he have a strategy he needs to share with Cleopatra?

→ *To tell your captain of Antony's request, turn to page 86.*

→ *To ignore what you heard, turn to page 87.*

"Antony needs our help," you tell your captain. Antony takes his flag and leaps onto your ship. Your boat and a few others break through the blockade of ships and chase after Cleopatra's squadron.

As you look back at the battle, you see that the Egyptian force is greatly outnumbered. You wonder what the other soldiers will think as they see Antony leave them to a losing battle.

Your ship escapes, but it will not be long before Antony is captured. Cleopatra and Antony refuse to be kept as Octavian's prisoners. They take their own lives. Octavian makes Egypt part of the Roman Empire, and you become part of the Roman Army. But there are not many wars left for Rome to fight. It is a country at peace for as long as you live.

THE END

To follow another path, turn to page 11.
To read the conclusion, turn to page 101.

You ignore Antony's request. You would rather die fighting for Egypt than run away like some coward. You are about to fire an arrow at a Roman boat when a flaming log hits your ship. The ship catches fire. You look at the water. Dead bodies and injured sailors are floating wherever you look.

"Over here!" a sailor shouts. You grab your spear and follow him onto the deck of a nearby Roman boat. You kill as many Romans as possible. But the effort is not enough. You are outnumbered. A Roman sailor stabs you in the chest with his spear. You slump to your knees. As you take your final breath, you hope the gods will reward you in the next life.

THE END

To follow another path, turn to page 11.
To read the conclusion, turn to page 101.

You are a servant to Queen Cleopatra. It is morning and time to dress the queen. You enter her chamber carrying robes of linen and wraps of soft silk. You have served the queen for many years, but her palace still amazes you. The walls are made of marble. The ceilings are coated in gold. Wide porches overlook lush gardens, fountains, and the city of Alexandria.

Charmian, another servant, arrives with the queen's makeup box. Charmian puts eye paint on the queen while you bring in her best wig. Tiny gold threads are woven in the hair. Small stones and glass trinkets are attached to a band in the front.

That night, Cleopatra throws a grand party in the palace. You make sure she has everything she needs. More wine. More figs. The party goes long into the evening, but you have plenty of time to enjoy yourself as well.

Queen Cleopatra had servants who attended to her every want and need.

The next morning, you go to wake the queen. But she is already up and pacing. "I must travel to Mark Antony," Cleopatra tells you. "He will battle with Octavian soon. He needs more supplies." You help Cleopatra pack. "A squadron of 60 ships waits in the harbor. I will travel with them to Actium in Greece." Cleopatra asks for volunteers to travel with her. The rest of the servants will stay behind and care for the children.

→ *To stay with the children, turn to page* **90**.

→ *To go with Cleopatra to Actium, turn to page* **94**.

You decide to stay with the children. After many weeks, Cleopatra returns to Alexandria with her squadron. You greet her at the harbor, where she declares a victory. The citizens of Alexandria celebrate, but you sense something is wrong.

"What really happened at the battle?" you ask, following her into the palace.

"We are doomed," she says, sitting down on a golden couch. "Antony's fleet surrendered to Octavian. Egypt's only hope is to beg Octavian for mercy."

Octavian's army is moving toward Egypt from the east. Cleopatra asks you to send her crown to Octavian. She asks him to crown one of her children as ruler of Egypt. Octavian refuses. He plans to make Egypt part of the Roman Empire.

Octavian arrives in Alexandria the following summer. You and Charmian help Cleopatra move armfuls of gold, silver, and jewels into the ground floor of her mausoleum. Then Cleopatra locks the three of you inside the tomb.

One day a servant arrives to tell Cleopatra that Antony is dying. He heard a rumor that Cleopatra was dead and fell on his own sword.

"Bring him to me!" Cleopatra cries. Servants carry Antony to the tomb. But Cleopatra refuses to open the door to the mausoleum. You and Charmian use ropes to pull Antony through a high window. He dies in Cleopatra's arms and is buried shortly after. Soon, Octavian posts guards outside the tomb. You are prisoners.

Turn the page.

Cleopatra is allowed to visit Antony's grave. At the grave site, Cleopatra tells you that Octavian plans to parade her through the streets of Rome.

"I can't let him take me alive," she explains. "Will you help me?"

"Of course," you answer. You sneak away from the grave. You arrange for a countryman to bring a poisonous snake to supper. Then you go to the palace to help Cleopatra bathe. As you are eating supper, a guard enters with a basket of figs.

"A gift from some poor countryman," the guard says. He hands you the basket and leaves. Hidden inside is the poisonous snake. The snake bites Cleopatra. She is poisoned and dies a short time later. You and Charmian allow yourselves to be bitten as well. You slump over and die. It is an honor to give your life for your queen.

Cleopatra was dead by the time
Octavian's guards found her.

THE END

To follow another path, turn to page 11.
To read the conclusion, turn to page 101.

You board Cleopatra's flagship and travel to Actium. It is a small coastal town in western Greece. When you arrive at Mark Antony's camp, his men are not doing well. There isn't enough food or fresh water for all of the men camped in the swampy bay. The men are sick with fever, vomiting, and diarrhea. Many have died. Antony does not have enough men to row his ships.

You are fanning the queen in her tent when Antony enters. He looks worried.

"I met with my commanders," Antony tells Cleopatra. "They agree a land battle is our best chance for victory."

Cleopatra shakes her head. "The Egyptian boats are bigger and stronger than Octavian's fleet. We must fight a sea battle." Antony agrees. He orders his empty ships burned so they can't be used against Egypt.

"We will not win this fight," Cleopatra tells you that night when you are alone. You load the royal treasure onto Cleopatra's flagship.

In the morning, Antony takes his fleet out first. They race out to the Roman ships, hoping to ram them apart. But Antony's men are too few and too weak. It is clear Antony will lose the battle. When the wind changes direction, Cleopatra calls for her squadron of 60 ships to make a getaway to the south. You and Cleopatra escape with the royal treasure.

You know it is better to save 60 ships than to lose them all. But you are afraid for Antony's men. Soon, Antony flees from the battle to join Cleopatra on her flagship. Her fleet makes it safely back to Alexandria. Thousands of Antony's soldiers die in the battle.

Turn the page.

Cleopatra met with Octavian
(left) in Alexandria. She
begged him for mercy.

The following summer, Octavian arrives
in Alexandria. His forces surround the palace.
Cleopatra surrenders her fleet to Octavian.
Antony's ground troops also surrender. Antony
stabs himself with his sword and dies in
Cleopatra's arms.

"I won't let Octavian parade me through the streets of Rome," Cleopatra tells you. She locks herself in her mausoleum with Charmian and another servant girl. You decide to stay in the palace and look after her children.

Several weeks later, Cleopatra takes her own life. You fear for the safety of Cleopatra's children, especially 16-year-old Caesarion. As Julius Caesar's son, he poses a threat to Octavian's power. Cleopatra set aside some of her treasure for Caesarion. She planned for him to escape through Ethiopia and head to India.

→ To help Caesarion escape, turn to page **98**.

→ To stay with the other children, turn to page **99**.

You help Caesarion pack the treasure and a few belongings. Then you sneak out of Alexandria and head toward Ethiopia. It is not long before one of Caesarion's tutors catches up with you.

"Octavian plans to make you king of Egypt!" the tutor tells Caesarion. "You must return to Alexandria at once."

When you arrive back in Alexandria, Octavian's guards capture you and Caesarion. Caesarion is put to death. Then you are beheaded for helping Octavian's enemy.

THE END

To follow another path, turn to page 11.
To read the conclusion, turn to page 101.

You stay in the palace with the other children, Alexander Helios, Cleopatra Selene, and Ptolemy Philadelphos. They are still young and need protection.

"I wish you a safe journey," you tell Caesarion as he makes his escape for Ethiopia.

After a few weeks, you learn that Octavian had Caesarion captured and killed. Soon, guards burst into the palace and take the remaining children. They are sent to Rome to live with Octavian's sister. You never see them again.

Octavian makes Egypt part of the Roman Empire. He pardons you and the citizens of Alexandria. You live the rest of your life in peace.

THE END

To follow another path, turn to page 11.
To read the conclusion, turn to page 101.

Today, the Rosetta stone is on display in the British Museum.

CHAPTER 5

ANCIENT EGYPT

Cleopatra was Egypt's last pharaoh. With her death, Egypt became a Roman province. The use of hieroglyphics disappeared. The worship of many gods ended as Christianity spread. Egyptians stopped preserving bodies and building large monuments to honor the gods. The secrets of ancient Egypt fell silent even to the Egyptians.

Then in 1799, French emperor Napoleon Bonaparte's army discovered what archaeologists call the Rosetta stone. They found it buried in the mud near Alexandria. The stone was an official document written in Greek and hieroglyphs. It honored the crowning of Ptolemy V Epiphanes, who ruled from 205 to 180 BC.

Howard Carter (left) discovered King Tut's tomb and mummy in 1922.

In 1822, French linguist Jean Francois Champollion deciphered hieroglyphic writing. The Rosetta stone served as a code breaker for historians. They were able to translate the hieroglyphs more accurately.

British archaeologist Howard Carter made another important discovery in 1922 when he found King Tut's tomb. The tomb still contained many treasures, including chariots, weapons, jewelry, clothing, and even food. Historians learned much about royal Egyptian burials by studying Tut's tomb, mummy, and treasure.

Unfortunately, many other ancient Egyptian mummies were taken home by tourists as souvenirs. Some were sold for medicinal purposes. Others were unwrapped so the linen cloth could be sold.

After more than 4,000 years, remains of King Khufu's pyramid still stand today. Named the Great Pyramid by historians, its polished bright white outer layer is mostly gone. Those stones were removed in later years to build other structures. Much of its contents had also been stolen over the years. Khufu's mummy has never been found.

Archaeologists continue to study ancient Egyptian ruins, artifacts, and literature. The harsh, dry climate of Egypt preserved much of its ancient history.

The ancient Egyptians were a highly advanced civilization. They developed a written language and created paper from papyrus reeds. They were also among the first people to use mathematics.

The ancient Egyptians had a superior knowledge of the human body. They wrote some of the world's first medical texts. Ancient Egyptian doctors performed surgeries and prescribed medicine. Some ancient Egyptian medical procedures are still used today.

In addition to medicine, the ancient Egyptians were pioneers in women's rights. Women held government positions. Some even ruled Egypt as pharaoh. Women could also own property, even if they were divorced from their husbands.

Ancient Egypt was one of the most exciting periods in history. With each new discovery, historians are one step closer to understanding the mysteries of ancient Egypt.

The Great Pyramid is the last remaining wonder of the Seven Wonders of the Ancient World.

Time Line

c. 3100 BC — Hieroglyphics is developed in ancient Egypt.

c. 2550 BC — Construction begins on King Khufu's pyramid. More than 2 million blocks of limestone are used to build his pyramid. It is completed 10 to 20 years later.

c. 1350 BC — King Akhenaten and Queen Nefertiti rule Egypt. They build the new city of Akhetaten and encourage worship of Aten, the sun god.

c. 1330 BC — Tutankhamen becomes king of Egypt at the age of 9. He dies around age 19.

332 BC — Alexander the Great conquers Egypt. He frees Egypt from Persian rule.

51 BC — Cleopatra VII becomes queen of Egypt at the age of 18. Her younger brother Ptolemy XIII rules alongside her.

49 BC — Ptolemy XIII drives Cleopatra out of Egypt.

48–47 BC — Cleopatra persuades Roman dictator Julius Caesar to place her back on the throne. Ptolemy XIII drowns in the Nile River. Ptolemy XIV becomes coruler. Cleopatra and Caesar have a son, Caesarion.

44 BC — Julius Caesar is murdered in Rome.

43 BC — Ptolemy XIV dies. Cleopatra names Caesarion as coruler.

41 BC — Cleopatra meets Mark Antony on her royal boat.

32 BC — The Roman Senate declares war against Cleopatra.

September 2, 31 BC — Octavian defeats Cleopatra and Antony at the Battle of Actium.

30 BC — Cleopatra and Antony commit suicide after Octavian takes over Egypt.

1799 — Napoleon's army discovers the Rosetta stone while digging a new fort near the Nile River in Egypt.

1822 — Jean Francois Champollion deciphers Egyptian hieroglyphs.

1922 — Archaeologist Howard Carter discovers King Tut's tomb in the Valley of the Kings.

2007 — King Tut's mummy is revealed to the world for the first time.

OTHER PATHS TO EXPLORE

In this book, you've seen how the events experienced in ancient Egypt look different from three points of view.

Perspectives on history are as varied as the people who lived it. You can explore other paths on your own to learn more about what happened. Seeing history from many points of view is an important part of understanding it.

Here are some ideas for other ancient Egypt points of view to explore:

+ Archaeologist Howard Carter discovered King Tut's tomb. What would it be like to uncover an ancient tomb and finally go inside to take a look?

+ Ancient Egyptian soldiers often had to be at sea or away from home for years at a time. What was life like for them?

+ Many citizens of Rome did not like Cleopatra. What would it be like to live in Rome when Cleopatra lived with Julius Caesar?

READ MORE

Blackaby, Susan. *Cleopatra: Egypt's Last and Greatest Queen.* New York: Sterling, 2009.

Burgan, Michael. *The Curse of King Tut's Tomb.* Mankato, Minn.: Capstone Press, 2005.

Leardi, Jeanette. *The Great Pyramid: Egypt's Tomb for All Time.* New York: Bearport, 2007.

Tyldesley, Joyce. *Egypt.* New York: Simon and Schuster Books for Young Readers, 2007.

INTERNET SITES

FactHound offers a safe, fun way to find Internet sites related to this book. All of the sites on FactHound have been researched by our staff.

Here's all you do:

Visit *www.facthound.com*

FactHound will fetch the best sites for you!

GLOSSARY

amulet (AM-yoo-let) — a small charm believed to protect the wearer from harm

archaeologist (ar-kee-OL-uh-jist) — a scientist who studies how people lived in the past

artifact (ART-uh-fakt) — an object used in the past that was made by people

hieroglyph (HYE-ruh-glif) — a picture or symbol used in the ancient Egyptian system of writing

mastaba (MAS-tuh-buh) — a rectangular tomb made from mud or stone

mausoleum (maw-suh-LEE-uhm) — a large building that holds tombs

palette (PAL-it) — a small case that held a scribe's tools and ink

pharaoh (FAIR-oh) — an Egyptian king

plague (PLAYG) — a disease that spreads quickly and kills most people who catch it

sarcophagus (sar-KAH-fuh-guhs) — a stone coffin; the ancient Egyptians placed inner coffins into a sarcophagus.

sickle (SIK-uhl) — a tool with a hook-shaped blade on a short handle used for cutting grain

BIBLIOGRAPHY

Carter, John M. *The Battle of Actium: The Rise and Triumph of Augustus Caesar.* New York: Weybright and Talley, 1970.

David, Rosalie. *Handbook to Life in Ancient Egypt.* New York: Facts On File, 2003.

Hodel-Hoenes, Sigrid. *Life and Death in Ancient Egypt: Scenes from Private Tombs in New Kingdom Thebes.* Ithaca, N.Y.: Cornell University Press, 2000.

Lehner, Mark. *The Complete Pyramids.* New York: Thames and Hudson, 1997.

Reeves, Nicholas, and Richard H. Wilkinson. *The Complete Valley of the Kings: Tombs and Tresaures of Egypt's Greatest Pharaohs.* New York: Thames and Hudson, 1996.

Smith, Craig B. *How the Great Pyramid Was Built.* Washington, D.C.: Smithsonian Books, 2004.

Time-Life Books. *What Life Was Like on the Banks of the Nile: Egypt, 3050–30 BC.* Alexandria, Va.: Time-Life Books, 1996.

Tyldesley, Joyce. *Cleopatra: Last Queen of Egypt.* London: Profile Books, 2008.

Tyldesley, Joyce. *Judgement of the Pharaoh: Crime and Punishment in Ancient Egypt.* London: Weidenfeld & Nicolson, 2000.

INDEX